DON'T ALLOW YOUR SCARS TO DETERMINE YOUR DESTINY

DUSTIN K. WISE

DON'T ALLOW YOUR SCARS TO DETERMINE YOUR DESTINY
ISBN: 978-0-9815379-7-9
Copyright @ 2010 by
Dustin Wise
P.O. Box 3603
Broken Arrow, OK 74013

Published by A & A Publishing
P.O. Box 324
Broken Arrow, OK 74013
(918) 459-6981

Text Design by: Bobby & Lisa Simpson
www.simpsonproductions.net

Printed in the United States of America.
All rights reserved under International Copyright Law. Contents and/or cover may not be reproduced in whole or in part in any form without the express written consent of the Publisher.

Contents

Introduction 5

Chapter One: What Are Your Scars? 7

Chapter Two: Realize Who You Are 19

Chapter Three: Reach Out 27

Chapter Four: Just Speak It 37

Chapter Five: Keep Dreaming 47

Chapter Six: Ignite Your Vision 57

Chapter Seven: Your Future Looks Better Than Your Past 65

Introduction

You may have picked up this book for one of several reasons. Perhaps you or someone you know has suffered from a scar that is either internal or external. Maybe you or someone you know is in need of comfort and motivation that may bring hope and light to the situation. Or maybe you judged the title and cover and thought, "Hey, this sounds good, I think I will get it!" Whatever it is, I am glad that you picked it up. I want you to use the same interest that caused you to start reading as the fuel to keep you on our journey together throughout this book.

While reading this book; you will find that no matter what has happened in the past that affected you in a negative way will not matter now. Your future is not determined by your issues. It doesn't matter how big you think your problem is, or what you went through last year, last month, last week, or even last night. There is nothing too big that God cannot fix. My point is, what has happened or is currently happening cannot determine the things that the Living God has predestined for you. The past may look dirty and cloudy, but you should not be looking back anyways. The Bible says to press on towards the goal by looking forward not backwards. That is what this book is going to teach, the future is bright.

Each chapter in this book is designed to help fight the daily battles from the past. As you read this motivational book, you will be given the opportunity to learn from the past. In doing so ignite the vision God has given you. Reaching out to bigger and better things that are in front of you, speak to the impossible situations and know your rightful place in Christ.

YOU ARE CAPABLE. That is right, more than capable, of achieving more than you could ever imagined by putting any scars, hurt, discouragement, or negative words behind you. So whatever you think your disqualifications are, forget about it. I do not want you to read this book with doubts about yourself. I believe in you, YOU ARE CAPABLE. Let us begin the journey together.

"Brethren, I count not myself to have apprehended: but this one thing I do, forgetting those things which are behind and reaching forth unto those things which are before." (Philippians 3:10)

Dustin K. Wise

Chapter One

What Are Your Scars?

A scar is your skin's way of repairing itself from injury. Look at your skin. You probably have one or two scars already. Most people do. Why? Because a lot of things leave behind scars — from falls, accidents, injuries, tests, trails or tribulations. Scars are a part of life and they often show what it is you've been through. For some people, scars are special. A kid in your class growing up might have had a scar on his chest because he had heart surgery as a baby. Or you might have a scar from the chicken pox. Centuries ago, warriors showed off their scars as symbols of their bravery and to impress their friends with the exciting tales about how each marking came to be. Nevertheless, different types of scars represent different things. .

Do any of your scars have a story? I am sure you do, there is not a scar without a story. Figuratively speaking, I personally believe that your scar may be perceived as the test that became the testimony. As cliché as that may sound, I am a firm believer in healing and growth. When many people think of a scar usually the first thought is often of someone falling and hurting themselves and then a bandage is used to cover the cut or wound. Let's dig a little deeper than that because believe it or not, every day, someone is dealing with a scar that is still healing—and a scar that reminds the person of the incident that may have caused the scar. **The scar is the reminder.** Where people are involved, there are always going to be examples and residue of scarring. Many people have turned those incidents in for the positive and many times — some are still dealing with the negative effects.

Scars cannot be classified for certain persons, or people groups and they do not respect one's race, ethnicity, sex or religion. Every one has been hurt somehow, whether it be the person sitting next to you on the bus, the cashier at your local grocery store, maybe even one of the ushers at your local church. Situations in life that may cause scarring happen to every one. Now some scars may appear bigger than others but regardless of size it is still considered a scar. There are personal scars, hidden scars, physical scars, emotional scars, spiritual scars, scars of abuse, scars of divorce, scars of rejection, scars of losing a child or parent and countless other types of scars.

There are so many scars that can be classified into different areas and categories but at the end of the day you cannot allow your scar to control you! You have to allow yourself to see beyond your scars and your hurts.

Some scars are tangible and others are intangible. Many others are visible as well as invisible. Either way you wish to classify it, it is key that you remember that there is still purpose residing on the inside of you. *We all are destined to live a purposeful life, find out what your purpose is and pursue it.* When you completely discover your purpose, the things of this world won't be able to hold you back or down any longer! In the journey of discovering my purpose, one of the things that I was reminded of was that when Jesus went to the cross he was aware of all that he would suffer; but since He knew what His purpose was He was able to stand strong. He looked past the name-calling and the belittling statements that would ensue from the people that He would die to save. He even looked past the beatings that would tear into His flesh—because *Jesus knew His purpose*. What is your purpose? Each and every one of us has a purpose that must be fulfilled throughout our lifetime on this earth but often we can allow those things that have hurt us distract us from our purpose. As long as you are determined to stay focused on the purpose in front you *it shall be fulfilled*.

You can Move on

The next few lines you will be reading are from a very good friend of mine, who has experienced many different scars, but she was determined not to allow what she experienced to determine where her life would be headed. I believe that as you read her story and learn about the different challenges and obstacles she was faced with, it will bring you great hope to your situation. I now turn your attention to Kiki.

"Please allow me to introduce myself to you, my name is Vo Thi Nhat Huyen but I would prefer to be called Kiki. I know Kiki doesn't have any similarity to Huyen but people will never be able to properly pronounce my Vietnamese name. I am not the typical eighteen year old girl but I am happy because of that. During the course of my life, I have experienced so many things that no one can ever imagine or think. Of course there were happy moments but there were many tough times as well. Nevertheless, I have no regrets. I appreciate all those moments and I am so grateful to have been able to experience each and every situation as it was given. It's a cliché but I truly believe that these experiences shaped me into the person I am today: strong, ambitious, persistent, resilient, and much

more…Well, I was born in a village, quite south of Vung Tao. Technically, I was born in a pig pen (no worries, I turned out quite fine despite the situation that I was born in). My parents were farmers who grew vegetables, fruits, coffee beans, and tended pigs for a living. I was their first child so they were really happy when they saw me squiggling around in the pig pen. During the first few years of my life, everything was awesome. Just a year and four months later, my mother gave birth to my younger sister, Nhi, whom I became best friends with until now. Life was going as happy and according to my parents' plan. And soon, more siblings were born and they were all girls, which made my parents a little bit sad but eventually they got over it. They really wanted a boy to continue the last name. So Nhi, Nham and then Thuong were born just a few years after the other. We were a happy family despite the fact that we had to work very hard for everything we had.

At the age of seven I had adapted strong work ethics around the house. A typical day for me would consist of the following: I had to wake up around six each morning to study, help mother cook and prepare breakfast, and then get ready to go to the field to tend vegetables and coffee beans by eight. I was working and sweating long hour of the days, going to bed and waking up and doing it all over again. There was no schooling available to my sisters and I. The only educations we received were when out parents sat us down and taught us. My father during lunch break and weekends, made my sister Nhi and I study Vietnamese repeatedly. I was young and hated him for doing that because I couldn't go out and play like the other kids in the neighborhood. Now looking back, I am really sorry for being such a grumpy young kid who didn't realize my father's good intention for my sisters and I. That was the life we had. We didn't have much luxury. No light, no electricity, no television or even a radio, but we were happy for we were a complete family: a caring mother, a loving father, three playful siblings and a vivacious me. I still remember those good memories we had together as a family. For instance, when the Lunar New Year came, my mother would dress us up in nice clothes and send us off to neighbors to get red envelopes. Those nights, we would stay up very late, telling traditional stories about our cultures and out families. I could never forget those memories even though I was just a child then. That is just one of many stories I have to share with you.

There was one terrible night in 2000 that changed the course of my life forever. I still remembered it was around seven o'clock at night when most of the village people already have gone to bed. My sister, Nhi and I were still studying some Vietnamese that my father had taught us. Since there was no electricity in the village, we were using a kerosene lamp as our source of light. My caring mother who saw how we needed the portable electric bin from the village shop, hurry went and started pouring a type of liquid into a bottle right in front of the doorway so she could use the moon as a source as light. Curious, Nhi, along with Thuong- who wanted to follow us- and I went and see what Mom was pouring. Nhi saw how she needed the light, quickly bent down with the kerosene lamp in her hand and asked what my Mom was doing. Unfortunately, Nhi didn't know that my mother was pouring gasoline so my father could go to the electric shop to get our electric bin for us to study. Before my mother could stop Nhi, the fire started. All three of us sisters were so frighten that we ran back inside the house. My Mother couldn't just run out so she ran inside with us. Soon, Panic arose all over my sisters and I. My mother saw her children slowly suffocating from the smoke; she rushed over and used her arms to shield us. As we laid there squirming in her arms, all we did was cry. Fortunately, before long, my brave father jumped in and rescued us. From the incident, eighty-five percent of our bodies were burned. We were immediately put into the hospital for six months. During these few months, there was an overwhelming pain all over our bodies. I could literally feel my skin being stripped off of my body and me screaming and begging the doctor to stop. As awful as the experiences were, they weren't as horrible as the news that my aunt brought us. As she stood in front of my bed weeping, I knew in my heart something terrible happened. However, I was taken by surprise when she announced that my mother had passed away in the hospital due to her severe burns. At that second, I thought everything was over. My mother had risked her life to save us. Tears kept rolling down my face and all I thought then was, 'I'm so sorry, mommy'.

That was a process, it took time to heal, and continue living life without my mother in life. It was a scar that I had to deal with and learn how to keep pushing through in order, to keep our family strong. The remaining of my father moved to California where we received treatment and where we relocated. Things were beginning to get back in order, life wasn't the same without my mother but it was starting to become as good as it possibility could. The pain was starting to heal and ease up until my father became sick and one night he was in need of going to the doctor, so I took him into the ER and I stayed up all night with him. He was in so much pain because of his liver cancer but he still managed to put on a brave face. I was studying for the SAT that night but it was just so uncomfortable sitting beside his bed in the ER that he scooted over and allowed me to lay on the end of the bed. As I cuddled there trying to get some sleep, I still remember him patting me on the head telling me "honey you can do it" simple as those words were made, they meant so much to me for he barely spoke due to the unbearable pain he was experiencing. In all the pain he was in he still had hope in me and uplifted my spirit because he knew that I was destined for success. Just two days after that ER night, my father's heart stopped beating. I was the first to receive the call from his doctor, stating that he was no longer on oxygen or a heart monitor machine. I thought that was good news since it indicated that he had improved. However, I was shocked when the doctor immediately announced to me afterward that it was because he had passed away in his sleep. No words could describe how I felt at that moment. I dropped to my knees and all I could do was panicked and cried. I remember crying so much that my eyes were red and I felt as if the world was falling apart, and there was nothing I could do. As I tried to get a grip of the situation, I discovered that I will never ever see my father again. He will never be able to attend my high school graduation like he promised me he would. Tears just kept rolling uncontrollable down my face. After crying continuously for more than an hour, my sister showed up. I was forced to break the news to them; they all shattered to the ground after looking at our father's body just lying motionless. Nhu (Mimi), the youngest, cried the loudest, with so much pain in her voice. She just kept calling our father's name just in case *he would awaken. My only thought was my father who never fancied anything luxurious or even took care of his own health had just died. At that point all five of us sisters thought that our world was over without our father. After losing my mother, he became the fire that was holding us together and without him, we felt as if the cold air would crush us all. My only question to life was what do I do now, where do I go.*

So many events have occurred since my father has passed away. Despite the fact that I have lost both of my dear parents, I'm still thriving and staying strong for many reasons. I will remain resilient to pay a tribute to my parents who had sacrificed their lives to my sisters and my success. I know for a fact that they want me to continue pursuing my dreams and just never give up!

Before my father passed away, he worked at several odd jobs to earn money to support the family. I remembered he was a janitor, a reconstruction worker, a lawn mower, and more. Throughout most of these jobs, my father was being insulted but he managed to keep his head held high with pride because of us. Regardless of how shameful cleaning the restroom or scrubbing floor might seem to people, to my father, it was a chance for him to earn money to save for his daughters to go to college and attain their dreams. Each penny he earned, he saved it up in a jar, hoping that one day he could send me and my sisters off to college. From his diligence, I started to work very hard as well. I wanted my father to be proud of me. I started to volunteer and be a part of the community. I volunteered at events such as "Youth Against Hate Crime Forum", "Third Thursday Art Walk," and more. I have also volunteered at Shriners Hospital for Children,

*South Sacramento Coalition for Future Leaders, Citizen for Fire Safety, and more. Because of my dedication and volunteerism to my community, I was Youth of the Month for Sacramento. I was truly happy and honor for this award but the reason that I volunteered a lot wasn't just because I wanted acknowledgement. The reasons I wanted to help out were first of all, the community has always been there to support my family since we first moved here so it's really rewarding to be able to give back. Also, it's a great way to help others while helping myself grow stronger as a person. Through helping others out in time of need, I learn to see life in a new light and appreciate everything even though when things are not going according to plans. I learn that even though I'm a burn survivor who had been through so many dramatic incidents, **it's all up to me on how I react to it. I can let all the negative things affect me or I simply just ignore them.***

Dreams are attainable to me. My dream is to become a motivational speaker. For the first five years after I got injured, I avoided social interactions as much as possible including school dances or sport games. I thought of myself as Frankenstein; I just wanted to die. I was just ashamed of this new me. However, after two years of continuous help from support groups and going to several burn camps, I went through a metamorphosis. I was no longer ashamed at my scars. I realized that my scars were what made me unique and special. I will use them as a testimony to show how letting go of the past has given me an incredible strength to achieve great things and that they can do the same. I want them to be proud of their scars and realize that they are strong and courageous burn "survivors", not "victims." As for any burn survivor or anyone who is currently suffering from a scar out there who might be reading this: I know the pain, the anguish, and the tears that you guys have been through. However, I was able to erase those negative emotions after I accepted myself for who I was really, and what God has created me to be. You see, when I was a junior, I was still not fully confident with myself yet and the junior prom was around the corner. I wanted to go and experience the event that many teenagers get to experience. However, in the end I did not get the courage to do that because I feared my peers would laugh at the scars when I wear the dress. However, this year as a senior, I will not let that fear bother me. I will go to prom and wear a cute dress without worrying about what others say. What I'm trying to say is that please don't let the precious time in your life pass by because of your scars. Enjoy life to the fullest and let go of the painful memories. Instead, start building a new road for yourself with vision full of happiness."

As you have just read about my dear friend Kiki's story you see how she has had the opportunity to allow her scars to distract her from her God's given destiny. She faces emotional challenges day in and day out. One of the things that separates Kiki from many other is that she hasn't allowed her scars to become attached to her. Kiki knows who she is, and since she knows who she is in Christ she is aware of power she has over any depression and fear from moving forward. She refuses to allow her emotions to control her. One of the most important things that are always good to know and remember is know who you are. Who you are has nothing to do with what you have experienced, or encounter, but with what you are destined for. And God has created each and every one of us to reign; we have been destined to reign over every problem, scar, hurt, pain, and situation. When we really fully understand who we are from the inside out, then and only then we can become and live life away from the past.

Some things are going take longer time to heal than others—so how do we deal with these situations? The key is to see yourself past all of the hurt, harm, pain, devastation, reject, guilt or whatever else. As you envision this, things will begin to seem better and your days will become brighter. **It will be hard to visualize it at first but just remember you've got to see it, before you see it, or you will never see it.** Start seeing yourself today full of purpose, destined for success and the past behind you.

Chapter Two

Realize Who You Are

Don't allow others to steal your identity

Do you know anyone who tries so hard to get close to someone, but the person they are trying to get close to doesn't give them any time or attention? It seems as if it might even be a one-way street. An important lesson I've learned in life is not to waste my time and energy on others who do not wish to like me or accept me for who I am. That's precious energy that is being wasted. It is energy being used negatively when it can be changed and used positively. **To live in total victory, then we have to accept the fact that not everyone is going to like us or agree with us.** Not every classmate, employer, friend or co-worker placed in your life are to become best friends with you. I have known people that have spent years and years trying to win the approval of someone else by sacrificing their own identity and goals in an effort to impress or win over one of their critics. The problem is, that person is never going to give them their approval. An interesting statistic I saw said that 25% of the people you meet won't like you and never will; 25% won't like you, but could be persuaded to; 25% will like you but could be persuaded not to; and 25% will like you and stand by you no matter what. Life gets a lot freer when we realize, "If this person doesn't like me, if they don't want to become my friend, if they aren't willing to give me the time of day then it's not that big of a deal. I realize they're one of the 25% that are never going to like me. I could compliment them every hour, send them flowers every day, mow their lawn every week, but this person still might never like me. Here's the key: don't waste your valuable time and energy playing up to them and trying to change their mind. Those are distractions. **You don't need their approval to be who God has made you to be.** When you are applying for different schools, jobs or internships you normally have to wait to receive the interview, letter or call stating that you have been accepted. Many times people get so caught up waiting on the phone call and forget that from self-evaluation and mirroring your life to the Word of God is where true satisfaction comes. You can be sure that you don't need an acceptance letter to do or become what God has called you to be. When you choose to look past the disapprovals of others and refuse to get involved in battles that don't matter , then God will not only send you people that accept and approve you, but He'll also send people that celebrate you, your talents, your personality and your accomplishments. They will love you for who you are. You won't have to constantly try and prove yourself by walking on eggshells and hoping that you're good enough. You can just relax and be who God made you to be, and they'll think you're the greatest thing in the world.

When I was growing up, in my mother's eyes, I could do no wrong. When things would go wrong at school my mother would say, "Not my little Dustin." "It may have been one of the other students who started this, but I know Dustin would never do that." The principal used to get so aggravated! They'd say, "Mrs. Wise thinks Dustin is a saint." She knew me and wanted the best for me no matter the situation. The way my mother thought about me is the same kind of friends that God wants to send your way. No matter the situation is or what comes against you they will be there pulling you out and always thinking, wishing, praying and believing the very best about you. No matter what the season is, they are going to be there to support, uplift and encourage you.

Based off of personal experiences, I personally believe one reason people will never accept someone for who they are, is because they're so insecure about themselves. They'll never give a compliment, or let you in their group because they're intimidated and threatened by you. The way they express that insecurity is to try and push you down so they will look bigger. They try to minimize you so they can equalize. They will try to diminish who you are, what you have to offer, and your accomplishments so they won't look so small. You're never going to change people like that. That's a battle that's not worth fighting. If you'll let it go, God will bring people into your life that add value rather than take it away, people that will be happy for you when you succeed.

I recently fell in love with a movie entitled To Save a Life; it is a must see movie. I am not going to give the whole movie away, just bits and pieces. The story is about someone who gets rejected and feels as if his life is no longer worth living. He feels as if no one is hearing him or paying any attention to him. His childhood best friend leaves him to be a part of the cool kids in high school and out of frustration he kills himself because no one was hearing his cry. Though he reached out to many people, it was to no avail. One of the problems that he faced was people around him would call him out of his name, belittling and lowering his self-esteem. His identity began to fall in the hands of his peers, as they continued speaking nothing but rude and ungodly statements into and over his life. He became uncertain as to who he really was and what he was capable of doing and accomplishing. His classmates refused to accept him for who he really was. They judged based on his clothing and the way he walked due a childhood accident. He didn't feel any loved by anyone. But in the mist of all of his turmoil there was a man with his arms stretched out wide and calling his name. That man is Jesus. He was with him every step of the way, even when the world was rejecting and putting him down. If he knew that, would his life have had a different ending? You may know someone who is going through the same, or better yet it might be you going through it. Regardless, you are always loved and nothing can or will take the love of Jesus Christ away from you. Today I am encouraging you to share the love of Jesus the Son of God, to someone around you. Always be a helping hand and care about those around you. After watching To Save a Life, I decided to make a bold change and not treat others a specific way based on where they came from, what they have or what they look like. I am sure we all are guilty of doing this one time or another. And if you have never done it than you have for sure thought it. The point is, we never know what someone is going through. Always try to help and offer your services to them. Whether it is your time, treasures or talents, be a resource to those who have no other source. Walk in love and show the love of God to those around you. You never know whose life you could be changing just by handling each and every situation out of love.

Who are you?

Sometimes things that scare us can become us. Take for instance this statement that I hear often, "I'm claustrophobic".

Taken from http://en.wikipedia.org/wiki/Claustrophobia:

Claustrophobia is typically thought to have two key symptoms: fear of restriction and fear of suffocation. A typical claustrophobic will fear restriction in at least one, if not several, of the following areas: small rooms, locked rooms, cars, tunnels, cellars, elevators, subway trains, caves, and crowded areas. Additionally, the fear of restriction can cause some claustrophobics to fear trivial matters such as sitting in a barber's chair or waiting in line at a grocery store simply out of a fear of confinement to a single space. However, claustrophobics are not necessarily afraid of these areas themselves, but, rather, they fear what could happen to them should they become confined to said area. Often, when confined to an area, claustrophobics begin to fear suffocation, believing that there may be a lack of air in the area to which they are confined. Any combination of the above symptoms can lead to severe panic attacks. However, most claustrophobics do everything in their power to avoid these situations. People who normally suffer from this normally become identified as a claustrophobic individual.

Just like many other things, this can be consider a scar, and a person can become so caught in up what they are being called, that it sticks to them and it becomes difficult to remove. However, do not allow that scar or hurt to become your identity. One story from the Bible that we can often look back at and reflect on someone being identified would be Blind Bartimeaus. This story is found in Mark 10:46. It speaks of a blind man, who sat by the wayside begging everyone for money; but many walked passed him with disgusted looks on their faces. The story goes on and Blind Bartimeaus was healed after he cried out to Jesus, "Have mercy on me!" Jesus healed him and stated your faith has made you whole. What a testimony! His faith made him whole. There is so much that can be pulled out of that story; but I want to focus on how Blind Bart became identified by his clothing. I can just see him now sitting there day in and day out waiting to get his healing. If this were to take place in this day and time, he would be considered a hobo. According to the Webster dictionary, "a hobo is a migratory worker or homeless vagabond, often penniless." I am sure Blind Bartimeaus was called everything but called of God, which could have possibly allowed him to forget who he was and where his identity came from. I believe many of us actually often face the same thing Blind Bartimeaus faced. We may not be blind or homeless but nevertheless, we have allowed every negative comment or slur to determine who we are. *I want you to forget about everything you were called and focus on what Jesus thinks of you.* In the eyes of Jesus, He has labeled us a child of the Most High God. We are the head and not the tail, we are above and shall never be beneath, we are Leander's and shall never become borrowers. He sees us healed, out of poverty and poverty mentality. He took away all of our sin and became sin and became sin, we now stand in Righteous standing due to that. When he sees us, he also sees righteousness. We are righteous because of the blood of Jesus. Even when you don't feel like it, just know you are. We can't go by feelings but by what we know and believe.

After my burn incident I was so ashamed of my scars and my marks that were left on my body. For a whole year I refused to run track and when the coaches asked me to run again it was even harder. My scars were hidden, so the only time someone would see them is if they were reviled. One day another student and I had gotten into a heated conversation and at the end of the conversation he made a statement that hurt me so much. Out of anger he went on and called me a burnt biscuit. After that statement was made I allowed my scars to become my identity and I felt as if I wasn't worthy or destined for anything. For years I fought that fight, it was all keep and hidden inside of me. So one day in conversation with my mother she had made a powerful statement to me, and she said Son your scars are beautiful and I thought to myself there is no way she could be saying this to me right now. She continues to talk and speak positively into my life and ensured me that out of millions of people living I am wearing those scars. She also told me that I should wear them with boldness and where them proud. One of the things that she said to me was that the scars that I wear, in God's sight is beautiful. From that day on, I started to look at my scars in the mirror with a different attitude. I reminded myself of who I was, and that what happened to me can't determine who I am or what I should be

I want to encourage you if there is something that you are allowing to identify you, that doesn't line up with the way God has intended for you to be identified than we need to work on changing it. You don't need to wait for others to tell you what they of think of you, tell yourself who you are in Christ. It is very important to declare with your mouth who you are in Christ because by the words of your mouth, you will put yourself at an advantage or disadvantage. I was taught that by meditating on the word God, we are transformed or reprogrammed to think positively. Here are some great confessions to make stating with who are you are in Christ.

- I am a child of God and a member of God's family.
- I am the righteousness of God in Christ.
- I can do what the Bible says I can do.
- I am who the Bible says I am, I have what the Bible says I have, I can never go under because I'm living on top.

Those are just a few things that you can start confessing that can change and rearrange your thoughts, your decisions and how to walk out what God has intended for you to walk out. Proper identification allows you to enjoy certain rights, benefits and privileges. Another important key that will help you grab all that has been destined for you to possess is reaching out to what is yours. You have to reach out to the things that are in front of you. In order to live the life and talk the talk you must also walk the walk. Walk it out by faith, reach out to impossible and know that what you have reached out for shall come to pass because of your willingness to reach. There is power when you reach out to the things that you know are yours. This is your day to take a stand and start being identified as God see's you and not your friends, co works, family or peers, and reach out the things that are in front of you. The best is yet to come.

Chapter Three
Reach Out

Have you ever been shopping and saw something that you knew you had to have? What did you do when you saw it? For some of us, it might have been a new coat, some shoes, a pair of jeans or maybe a piece of chocolate. In order for you to get what caught your interest, in order to find out if it was actually what it appeared to be, you have to reach out and grab it. Believe it or not reaching out and grabbing is actually easier than making the purchase on the item that caught your interest. That is the same way it is with the blessing that God has in store for you, they are already waiting on you and all you have to do is reach out and take a hold of it. . You have to look past your scar in order to reach out. Looking past your scars will enable you to receive all of the blessings and benefits that are available to you. All of God's promises are yes and amen.

    Let me use myself as an example, I love going into Express Clothing store and seeing what interests me the most. After I find just what I was looking for, I have to reach out and grab it. After that, I must continue to the checkout stand and make the purchase. At this point I either pay with check, bank card, credit card or maybe even cash. After doing that I wait while they bag up the item I just purchase and out the doors I go. The blessings that God has in store for us can be looked at with that same approach, but the only difference is that there aren't so many steps involved. To receive the blessing from God, all you have to do is reach out and once you have reached out and released your faith for the object, it shall come to pass. You must reach out to those things that are before you.

Three Keys on how to reach

Reaching is very important and here are a few keys that you can apply when reaching out towards the things that you are in need of the most:

First off, when reaching, you need to have **faith**, it takes faith to reach out towards something that you might not see. Luke 1:37 (KJV) states, "For with God nothing shall be impossible, another translation reads as this, for there is nothing which God is not able to do. What does that tell us? Once we release our faith for those things that are in front of us and expect God to move and turn our impossibilities into possibilities, then we shall receive exactly what we have believed for.

Secondly you need to have **courage**. Courage can also be defined as having *confidence*; you have to be confident of the things that are in store. A definition of courage is being able to deal with the situation you're against fearlessly. The key word in that definition was fearlessly. You must decide that no matter what the situation looks like, no matter how things are going or what is around you, you will approach the situation headfirst. All fear will leave and desist because your faith and confidence in what is in store. Courage can also be described as having the mind set or spirit that enables a person to face difficulties, dangers, pain or etc. without fear. Deuteronomy 31:6 (KJV) reads as follows, be strong and of a good courage, fear not, nor be afraid for the lord your God will be with you. I am here to inform you that courage is something that we all need to fight the good fight of faith. Once we grasp a hold of it and never let it go, the sky will become the limit. *All that God has in store for you is limitless and immeasurable.* We need to walk in courage in every area of our life. Once we start walking and living in courage, nothing will ever be able to bring about any fear or hold us back from the high calling God has placed in each and every one of us.

The third key to reaching out is **tenacity**. When I think of an animal that would best describe the characteristic of tenacity the best one that comes to my mind is a bulldog. A bulldog can best be described as a very affectionate and dependable animal, known for its courage and its excellent guarding abilities. They are determined, persistent and they refuse to give up easily. Once they grab a hold of something in a heated situation they then become very tenacious, grabbing pulling of something not letting go and unwillingness to give up, until it is completely demolished. After learning and studying the bulldog, I was thinking to myself, "How many things can we can get complete and achieve if we only had the mindset of a bulldog?" So that when the situations of life try and dominate our health, finances, school work, jobs or any or area of life we would stand strong and keep going forth. Like a bulldog, we would not let loose or lose sight but rather grab a hold of the promises of God and walk in that which He has called us to walk into.

Faith will enable you to activate the courage it will take you to be tenacious about what it is you would like to get and where you would like to go. (You may have to read that twice!) Never give up or quit. Quitting is easier than starting but if you apply the principles just giving you shall overcome each and every time and end up on the winning side.

My Story

Growing up, I always enjoyed being a helpful hand around the house by doing what I could that would be beneficial to my parents. One day after coming home from school, dinner was being prepared. The telephone rang so my mother went to answer it and asked me to watch the meat cooking on the stove. I began to stir the meat until I smelled an unusual smell. First, I checked the burner to see if something was stuck and needed removing. That wasn't the problem, so I lifted the pot to see if there was something stuck to the bottom of the pot. That wasn't the problem either, so I continued to go about what I was doing. After a few seconds, I glanced down at my shirt and I saw flames everywhere. The flames were uncontrollable and I panicked not knowing what to do or who to call for help. As the flames continued to grow, I felt the heat of the fire approaching my face. At this point, my oldest sister noticed and ran into the kitchen, not paying any attention as to where she was going. There was a pan of oil sitting on the edge of the counter. She accidentally hit the pan and the oil flew in the air and she slipped and fell flat on her back.

At this point and time the flames are just moving closer and closer and the heat is rising. I thought my life was coming to an end. I didn't know what I had done or what I was to do. In my thought I was sure death was to come. I then proceeded to lie down to burn and die. I thought all hope was gone and there weren't any more options. My mother then saw the fire on my shirt and ran into to help. Once I saw that, I ran in the opposite direction because I didn't want her to get hurt by any means. As I took off, she yelled and proclaimed with everything inside of her, "Devil you can't have my baby." I then felt a sense of relief as she reached out with everything she had in her. When she reached out, the shirt came right off my back; not over my head, or under my legs or through my arms but right off my back with all the original buttons still attached.

See, I was placed in a situation and my back was against the wall; I wanted to call for help and scream but I was stuck in a state of shock. I must admit it was one of the hardest things to go through and overcome but God gave me peace, grace and supernatural strength to overcome. Have you ever been placed in a situation where you didn't know what to do or who to call? You might have panicked and got frantic because you weren't certain of what the outcome would bring. I am sure that you can attest that you eventually overcame the wall that was in your way. You might not remember how, or all the steps you went through to get to where you are now, but I am sure I can tell you: It was God; He was with you coasting you through, holding your hand and even when you gave up on Him He stood right there waiting for you to return home.

I am sure you have heard the story about the walls of Jericho, and if you haven't it can found in the Joshua chapter 6. Hebrews 11:30 refers to the events at Jericho and it reads, "By faith the walls of Jericho fell down after they were encircled for seven days." The children of Israel believed God for victory; they refused to give up until that in which they believed for came to pass. For seven days they marched and released their faith and became tenacious about getting what was theirs, and on the seventh day the walls crumbled.

So the people shouted when the priests blew with the trumpets: and it came to pass, when the people heard the sound of the trumpet, and the people shouted with a great shout, that the wall fell down flat, so that the people went up into the city, every man straight before him, and they took the city. (Joshua 6:20)

Here we read that after the walls fell they went back and took everything the enemy attempted to take from them. Growing up in children's church that might have been one of my favorite bible stories. While I was in the hospital, I would sit wondering when my day seven was going to come and I was going to be able to do like they did and everything around me would turn around for my good. I would begin to get frustrated after day eight and nine but my situation wasn't changing, in fact it was getting worse. Looking back at what I am knowledgeable of now and what I wasn't so knowledge of then is life changing. See, I didn't have to wait until day seven for all of my pain to go away, to gain my appetite back and others things I believed for. All I needed to do was reach out by faith, courage and tenacity for what I believed for and surely it was mine. You might be like I was or have the mentality I once had, but I want to inform you of something; *you don't have to wait for seven days for your situation to change or walk around a building for you to see a different outcome.* All you have to do is know what you believe and believe what you know. Apply the principles given and more positive ones if you have any in mind and stand strong and believe for every circumstance.

While I was in the hospital everyday my mom would make the long drive to come and visit me. No matter what the doctors had to say once she arrived she made up in her mind that the best was still yet to come. It didn't matter the different surgeries they wanted to complete, or how much blood I had lost in the middle of the night; she always kept a positive attitude and never stopped speaking positivity. I was treated at the Grossman Burn Center, in Sherman Oaks, California. I suffered second and third degrees burn in hidden spots. Dr. Richard Grossman from the burn center considered me the miracle boy. Dr. Richard did amazing work on me. Since then I have had to return several times for steroid injections on the scars to prevent kiloids from growing on top of the skin. I often wonder what would it be like if my mom didn't reach out by faith. At that particular time she reached out and in spite of the situation she knew what the end was going to be. She reached out and stood firm on the promise of God.

When we stand on the word of God and stop paying so much attention to the problem then the promises are activated. Just as I was cooking on the stove and couldn't wait for the meal to be completed. I want you to close your eyes and picture yourself cooking. There should three major different seasonings sitting on the stove. One flavor can be faith, the other courage, with a big bottle of tenacity sitting behind them all. I want you to mix them all up together turn the stove up to its highest level and let them cook. As they are cooking you should just sit back and rest in the fullness of joy and believe that once it is ready to be served, it is going to be one of the best dishes you have ever cooked or experienced. Some problems might require more seasonings. *Just think of the larger the pot the more you have dash in there.* If you need peace, then throw some peace in there. Someone might need joy, the unspeakable joy, if so, add some joy. The point is no matter what is trying to hold you back or hinder you cook it up, stir it up and believe that once it is all said it done things are going to be better than when they first started.

Look past your limitations

I want to share a story with you about a woman in the Bible in Mark chapter 5; this particular woman had determination, perseverance and tenacity. This same woman was also very sick; she went from place to place seeking help. She went to every physician she could find. Though she traveled near and far from town to town looking for help that was not to be found. This woman wanted to be healed so badly that she even went out and spent every penny she owned. The Bible continues to tell us that she didn't get any better but as a matter of fact her symptoms worsened. One day as she in pain and not knowing what to do or who to go for help, she heard there was a healer in town by the name of Jesus. That very day she mixed her determination, perseverance and tenacity with faith. *That was the combination that changed her life forever.* The Bible says that when the woman heard that Jesus was in town, she said to herself, "If I can only touch the hem of His garment." One translation says, she kept on telling herself "if I could only touch the hem of His garment I shall be made whole." She was speaking from a place of faith. After fighting this sickness for twelve years I bet she was constantly encouraging herself and focusing on her healing, victory and that all her finances would get back in order. I could also see her wanting to give up and quit; I am sure she had mixed emotions. The Bible says that when she touched the hem of His garment, she was instantly made whole. Jesus then turned around and started inquiring as to who touched him. The touch he received from her was different than all the other touches he had been receiving all day. The woman spoke out and admitted to touching and Jesus said unto her daughter thy faith hath made thee whole. I believe it was a touch of faith; her faith healed her and drove out the disease that was in her body. Faith can move any mountain that tries to stand against you.

What I find so interesting is that this woman was definitely limited in her natural abilities. I am more than certain she was emotionally and physically a wreck. She definitely had no money and she was a woman—in those days, that was a limitation in itself. None of these things stopped her; she still stood still and was very determined to keep the faith. I am sure she fought fear, also *but she pressed past those limitations and pressed right into Jesus.*

I have a question for you—What are the limitations that you see in your life? Do you have sickness, relationships problems, financial lack or anything else that isn't pleasing to you or to God. Yes, you may have some limitations but just as the woman with the issue of blood pressed through and fought anything and everything that was limiting her; I believe you can do the same. You don't have to stay where you have been or be defined by your past. There is still hope for you this day, right now, this very second. I want to encourage you to find your determination perseverance, and tenacity mix them together with supernatural faith. Keep telling yourself: "I know I am going to make it." Speak from a place of faith just like she did. She didn't know the outcome but her faith did. See yourself healed, changed and as if the breakthrough has already taken place. Keep pressing past your limitations today because God has victory and wholeness in store for you in every area of your life.

Chapter Four

Just Speak It

"*And God said, Let there be light: and there was light. And God saw the light, that it was good: and God divided the light from the darkness. And God called the light Day, and the darkness He called night. And the evening and the morning were the first day.*" (Genesis 1:3-5)

God spoke light into existence on the first day. But as we look further in the first chapter of Genesis, we discover God spoke two other lights into existence on the fourth day:

"And God said, Let there be lights in the firmament of the heaven to divide the day from the night; and let them be for signs, and for seasons, and for days, and years: And let them be for lights in the firmament of the heaven to give light upon the earth: and it was so. And God made two great lights; the greater light to rule the day, and the lesser light to rule the night: He made the stars also. And God set them in the firmament of the heaven to give light upon the earth, and to rule over the day and over the night, and to divide the light from the darkness: and God saw that it was good. And the evening and the morning were the fourth day." (Genesis 1:14-19)

To break that down in a simpler form, it states "God Spoke." The book of Genesis continues to number all the other things that God spoke into existence. Here are even more examples of the power in God's words:

"And God said, let the waters under the heaven be gathered together unto one place, and let the dry land appear: and it was so. And God called the dry land Earth; and the gathering together of waters called the Seas: and God saw that it was good. God than said, let the earth bring forth grass, the herb yielding seed, and the fruit tree yielding fruit after his kind, whose seed is in itself, upon the earth and it was so." (Genesis 1:9)

Whatever God spoke it came to pass; it didn't matter what it was or how farfetched it might have seemed. At the end on the last chapter, we considered the concept of reaching out and looking past our hurt and scarring. I got a little ahead of myself but I wanted you as the reader to understand that even in all of that – in the scarring and reaching out, there are still a few more steps. Just speak it, is the next thing that I would like for you to consider. That is why I chose the passage in the book of Genesis to talk to you about speaking and the power that we possess in our words. I don't want to give the rest of this book away, but the Bible says that we are made in the image of God and if we possess the features and attributes of our God, then we too possess power in our words. And we will talk more in depth concerning that later. Let's get back to the power of speaking. Now after speaking over something you must release your faith in what you want to speak. The words you speak, when faith is released will cause your circumstance to line up – but you must speak from a point of faith and you must speak lining every word up to the Word of God. Some of you might be wondering what faith is, according to Hebrew 11:1 Faith is the substance of things hoped for, the evidence of things not seen.

That scripture was written out of the New King James, but in the New living Translation it reads like this, Faith is the Confidence that what we hope for will actually happen; it gives us assurance about things we cannot see. Lets break it down. When you speak over different things, situations or what you would will like to see come to past you must have the confidence that whatever was that was said from your mouth will actually happen. Webster's dictionary describes confidence as "a state of being certain either that a hypothesis or prediction is correct." When you speak you must be certain because uncertainty will lead to fear. **Once fear steps in then faiths steps out.** Pastor Kenneth Hagin Jr. says it best, "Faith and fear cannot reside in the same household." If you get to the point where you are allowing fear to enter in and rule your thoughts, actions and words, then faith goes out the window. If you choose to only allow faith in and stand on the promises of God, no matter the season, fear will remain outside looking inside at all of the blessing empowering you. Be encouraged today because the God of increase is on your side! As you stay in agreement with Him, you'll see His blessing, honor, and increase in every area of your life!

It's in your Tongue

Your attitude is controlled by your words. Right words will open the doors for God to bless you and wrong words will allow the enemy to come in and destroy you. John 10:10 (KJV) says, "The thief cometh not, but for to steal, and to kill, and to destroy." He can only do that if you allow him to and the easiest way to let him in is through your words. It continues in saying I (Jesus) has come that they might have life, and that they might have it more abundantly. What you speak can effect what you will accomplish in life. Never say what you can't do. I remember in elementary school my second grade teacher told the class a little story that has stuck with me all these years: This story was based on two best friends, their names were Can't and Won't. Everywhere Can't and Won't went nothing good worked out for them. Every time they were sent on a mission it always ended up as a mission failed. I can go on with the story but to chase to the point. **Cant is a dressed up word for won't. Whatever you say what you can't do, it is just a better way of saying what you refuse to do.** We should never live in that mentality. Never get caught up thinking what you can't do, or what abilities you don't posses to complete what needs to be completed. One Sunday morning, Pastor Hagin preached a powerful message entitled "Speak the Voice of Faith." It was very encouraging and a powerful message; it's amazing how when we just speak the voice of faith God will move on our behalf. Your faith is measured by the words you speak. You can say and believe all day but nothing begins to manifest until you speak. The more you speak the Word the more your spirit is filled with positive things, and I can assure you God is pleased. It's all in your words— defeat or victory, depression or joy, sickness or heath, poverty or wealth, it's all up to the words you speak. Proverbs 6:2 says, "You are snared by the words of your mouth, caught by the words of your tongue." Since we know we are going to be captive to the words that we decided to speak we might as well make them good words, words of encouragement, words that will benefit and harm us.

Speak Positively

One day I was out at lunch with a group of friends, and almost everything that was said was negative. Everything they said was hopeless. The reason they were speaking this way was because they had allowed their problems to speak to them. **Never let your problem speak to you. You need to stand strong and speak to the problem.**

When you speak to your problem know that what has been spoken shall come to pass. No matter how big, small, crazy, ugly or confusing your situation might be we must still always speak positive things over it. In English grammar we are taught that two negatives equal a double negative, and when you place two negative words in the same sentence it becomes grammatically incorrect. Example>I ain't gonna go to the mall because I don't have any money. In that sentence the negative words are ain't and gonna. If an English teacher were reading this, they would be highly upset because of the way the words are together. A double negative will never be changed unless you change one of them. If you aren't speaking anything positive how do you expect anything to become positive? If you speak positively over your negative situation or surroundings than things will began to change. The more positively you speak, the more convinced you will become about the situation changing. *Speak from the place of faith, as if it is already so.* You are a conqueror and you can conquer any and everything that stands against you. Just speak positively.

Proverbs 18:21 (KJV) tells us that Death and life are in the power of the tongue. If you speak *life* over your circumstances as opposed to death then life is what you will get. We need to use our tongue to bring words of life and encouragement to those around us and most of all ourselves. Did you know that you had the power to posses any and everything you are in need of or wanting? Well let me tell you a little secret: **YOU DO**, just speak to it. Your tongue can either break or make you. My first year in Oklahoma was such a shock to me because of the cold winter. Where I am from we don't have winter storms, ice storms or freezing weather. My body was not adjusted to the climate of the atmosphere. One day as I was getting ready for class I was feeling awful. I had a fever, running nose, red eyes and I could barely talk. Getting out of bed was not an option. I didn't know what was going on with me. I began to start telling everyone I was sick. I was forced to take days off of school and work. It seemed as if nothing was getting better for me. I went to the doctor and he prescribed me some medication. Well, to let the truth be told, that wasn't getting the job done either. At this point I didn't know what to do. One day a classmate called out of concern because they hadn't seen me in a while. I began to tell them what I was experiencing and how sick and uncomfortable I was. Well, she then pretty much slapped me in the face with just a few words. She said something along these line,. "The reason your situation hasn't changed is because of what you are speaking over it not only to yourself but also others." She told me I needed to start confessing my healing, regar*dless of what I was feeling*. When people started asking how I was feeling, my response changed from "I am sick" to "I am healed in the name of Jesus." I started to stand on Isaiah 53:5 which reads, "He was wounded for our transgressions, he was bruised for our iniquities, and the chastisement of our peace was upon him..." and now comes my favorite part of that scripture, "...with his stripes we are healed. . It doesn't say we are going to be, or in a few days, or next month or even after surgery, but it said we **are** healed. If I am healed than sickness can't enter into my body that has already been healed through my savior Jesus Christ. Once I got a hold of that and what it really meant, then 24 hours later I was HEALED!

I will never forget this powerful truth that I heard one Sunday. I was informed that **on my weakest day I am still stronger than the Devil on his strongest day**. That means so much as I thought about it, to that remember even when I was so sick that I couldn't talk, walk or move—I was still stronger. I still had the power to speak to my situation and know that by faith it was coming to pass. Some of us need to just think about that statement again. No matter how hard you have fallen, or how things look or feel. You still have the power. You can control how far the situation gets due to your tongue and what you are speaking and believing.

One of the most important things we can do to keep ourselves moving in the right direction is to carefully guard what we say. Remember, your words are seeds that produce the harvest of your future. If you go around speaking negative words of doubt and defeat, you are uprooting your harvest of blessing. You are literally speaking against what God wants for your life! But if you'll stay in agreement with the God of increase, if you'll declare His Word over your future, then you are setting yourself up to receive the victory and blessing God has in store for you. Start speaking right now, speak life, hope, peace, joy and watch it all come to pass.

Matthew 15: 10-11 Jesus said, "It is not that which goeth into the mouth defileth a man; but that which cometh out of the mouth, this defileth a man." The things we are allowing our mind to think on and our mouths to speak will defile who we are and what will become of our situation. In every situation and in all circumstances, speak the Word **only**. Three simple keys that will always produce what you are speaking are: Confession, Believing and Acting.

Whenever I think of confessions I think of it as of a law. A law is something that is set in place to help and protect others and ourselves around us. The most common traffic light consists of a set of three lights: red, yellow and green. When illuminated, the red light indicates for <u>vehicles</u> facing the light to stop. Yellow indicates caution because lights are about to turn green or because lights are about to turn red. The green light means to proceed only if it is safe to do so. There are some variations in the use and legislation of traffic lights and complex intersections may use any combination of these. But the ultimate understanding is always the same. What would happen if someone broke the law and ran a red light on accident? Unfortunately, they have to suffer consequences that they might not enjoy, be it receiving a ticket, paying fines or opening up the opportunity for an accident to occur. When we take heed of the traffic laws that are in place, then the roads are safer and all cars can stay intact without the possibility of an accident or outrageously priced ticket. All of this is due simply to obeying laws.

Now let's talk about the law of confession. The law of confession can be looked at in the same approach. It is guaranteed to work when operated correctly. The things that we choose to confess are the same things we will eventually possess. When you confess, believe and act on the word of God then the law of confession goes into effect. It can be said that the word of God works off of your last confession. Think to yourself what was my last confession? Did you give into the situation, did you confess what the doctor reports said, did you confess what you were feeling or looking like, or did you make a faith confession? It is good to hold fast to your confession of faith; the word will work off that confession.

According to Webster's dictionary, the definition of believe is to "have confidence in the truth, or the reliability of something without having absolute proof." Acting is defined as the act of doing something, or putting something into motion. The law of confession can also be seen as a traffic signal. The red light can represent your confession; the yellow light can represent what you believe. Acting upon what you are confessing and believing could be in representation of the green light. If you notice the green light stood for acting, which is for a reason. In order to receive all that God has in store for you, we must be in the go stage also know as motion, movement acting upon what the word says for our lives. Many times we can allow ourselves to get stuck at the red light also known as confession. Have you been to the place where you were confessing all day and night but the situation seems as if it wasn't changing, or the circumstances around you were still overriding your confessions? That is because you are still parked at the red light your situation or your problems aren't moving until you move them. In order to remove yourself from that red light or get out of the ditch you are currently in would be to starting believing what you are confessing. Someone might say well Dustin; I believe what I am confessing. My next question back to you would be, what are believing in your heart? Proverbs 23:7 (KJV) says, "as a man thinketh in his heart, so is he." What are the things you are thinking; not thinking good and positive things that line up with what you are confessing is just as bad as not believing. The more you confess positivity, the more your heart will become alert to the confession and your belief system will begin to change. In order to believe in something or someone it must be in your heart. It comes from your heart when you think about and act upon whatever it might be you believe.

The more we are confessing something the easier it will become for us to believe what we are confessing. Its like a little step system. What you are confessing will turn into your thoughts. Your thoughts will than turn into the words you speaks, the words you speak will turn into what you believe. What you believe will turn into what you will begin to act upon. What you are acting upon will than form your destiny.

Now just envision yourself driving, you just pulled up to traffic signal or problem. The light is getting ready to turn red, but it's in the yellow stage. At that point and time start your belief. Start believing the best. The light has just turn red, what are you going to do? You should start your confessions, speak to the problem and command that it goes. Make sure your confessions and believing are adding up to what is your heart. The light has just turned green, this is your chance go, go, go, go. You just did it; guess what that was a practice test. The real deal is yours to do. The next time you are faced with a red light and it seems as if nothing is changing or moving. See the light turning green, see your dreams coming to pass; envision the end of a difficult situation. The end is always better than the beginning. What scenic route will you take next? In other words, what are your dreams? What adventures would you like to take and have not yet had the opportunity to conquer? All the dreams that you had as a child, have you pushed them aside, or thought them to be foolish? Think on those things again and I encourage and implore you – keep dreaming.

Chapter Five
Keep Dreaming

Almost all of us have had dreams and visions that we desire to see fulfilled our lives. My question to you is *what happened to that dream?* Are you still focused on that dream, or have you turned your attention to others things that are not beneficial to you or the fulfillment of your dreams? These distractions could consist of fear, disappointment, rejection or self-pity. Often the people you surround yourself with can also hinder or hurt your dream. It's always good to be surrounded with positive people and better yet dreamers. If *distractions* or *relationships* have hindered your dreaming, today is your day to dream again, and not only to dream again, but also to actually start working toward that dream.

In writing this chapter my objective was for it to pump you up so much that you would continue to dream and begin to dream again if you have stopped. And as you are dreaming keep those dreams you dream in front of you. And also realize that no matter where you are in life, no matter what you have been through and no matter what is to come, you must keep dreaming and keep the dream alive... Never stop dreaming. I personally believe that everyone has a dream but not everyone's dreams comes to pass. Often this is because we refuse to act on our dreams and we never step out of our comfort zones. It's like having an old coat sitting in the back of your closet. You know that it is there and you think about it from time to time, but you never check on it to make sure it is in good condition or if it is still there. That is the way we can often treat our dreams, we think about them from time to time and that is about it.

As you read this next section, I encourage you to read Genesis 37.

In Genesis 37, there is a story about a man by the name of Joseph who had a dream. Not only did Joseph have dreams but He also *believed* in the dreams he encountered. Many times we can allow a dream, thought or idea to intimidate us, causing fear to rise up inside of us. Don't allow your dreams or visions to intimidate you. As you read this chapter, you will find out what Joseph went through and the many challenges he was faced with day in and day out, but Joseph never gave up on his dreams. Many of us have been in his position or might even in that position as of now. We think no one has it harder than us. We think no one understands our problem or cares to hear about what we are going through. I have breaking news for you! God was with Joseph every step of the way and the same God that was with Joseph through it all, is the same God that is with you. God never left Joseph, not even in his darkest hour, and that same God has and will never leave you. Isn't that comforting? Knowing that at all times I will have a comforter, protector, friend, father and brother: My God is all of that in one. He can and will be whatever you need Him to be whenever you Him to be it. He will be with you in you highest highs and lowest lows. **He believes in you and your dream and will be there with you ever step of the way.**

Believe in your dream

Sometimes the hardest thing for someone to do is believe. Believing is not always easy when you are always looking at your obstacles, circumstances, surroundings and negative relationships. Believe it or not, believing is one of the most important things we need to overcome and surpass whatever is holding us back. Joseph, in the book of Genesis, was a dreamer as you have already read; He was a man of many dreams. One of the things I love most about Joseph was that no matter how big the dream was that God had showed him, he never got afraid of the dream. Joseph stood firm and knew that there wasn't anything too hard for him to accomplish. What are you doing with the dream that has been sitting deep down inside of you? Are you afraid of it and possibly believe that it is impossible for someone like you to do? I've felt that way so many times; but the point is that we can't let fear hold us back.

2 Timothy 1:7 says, "For God did not give us a spirit of fear or timidity but a spirit of power, of love and of self-discipline." That is an excellent verse to mediate and stand on. I look over that scripture at least once a week to remind myself what God has given me. And since I know what I have been given I know that I have the ability to walk in and live out all of my God-given potential. It is very important to confess the Word over our life and our dreams. Personally, I remind myself of these Biblical truths: I possess the spirit of power to take down anything that tries to stand against me; I have wonder working power dwelling deep inside of me; I am powerful and cannot be defeated; I walk in love, even when things aren't going my way and someone upsets me.

As we start declaring and walking in the things we have been given, such as power, love and self-discipline it will become a habit and lifestyle that we engage in. Anytime something tries to contradict what the word of God says, we should choose to declare who we are and put all of our trust in what we are saying and believing

I've heard it said, "If your dreams aren't as big as the God you serve than you aren't dreaming big enough." What does that mean? That simply means that you should never dream small. *Your dreams should require the help of your God.* When you know that you cannot fulfill the dream all by yourself, you can be sure it is a God-given dream. Luke 1:37 says, "For with God nothing shall be impossible." Notice, it doesn't say "for certain dreams, or to a selected group of people." It says for *with* God. If God is involved in your dream, you know it can happen. That is so powerful. If you just put all your trust into the King of Kings and by faith know that it shall come to past, there should be nothing that can worry or discourage you. I strongly believe that only God can turn any impossible situation and make it possible, but first we have to believe. Choose to dream and believe big, and watch big things come to pass.

You can't tell everyone

It is essential that we are careful with whom we share our dreams or visions with. Not everyone is going to stand in full agreement for the fulfillment of the dream. My mother always said, "Not everyone needs to know what you are doing, or what God has given you to complete." Not everyone is going to stand fully behind you in what you want to get accomplished. *The last thing you need is someone who knows your dream, but doesn't believe in what you are dreaming.* I have a name for people with that mentality. They are dream-blockers; they block the dream you are dreaming from coming to pass. Do you have any dream blockers in your life? Dream-blockers will and can affect you in more ways than you know. They will begin to rub off on you, and you won't even know where it is coming from. *They will drain the dream right out of you.*

I personally believe that God places friends in your life for three different reasons. **Some come for a season, a reason and some are there for a lifetime.** The ones that come for a season were only meant to be there for a time of your life. They might have been there to help you overcome certain obstacles that you are faced with in life. Just like the seasons change after the appointed time, the friends that are there for a season should be there for the winter, but when summer comes if they are still in your life and not helping you put out *productively* than their season might be over. Know when the season is over and how to change from season to season. I am not saying be a friend hopper, but not everyone is made to travel and support your dream. You must know how to rightly divide your friends and understand what they were placed in your life for.

The friends who are there for reasons are the friends who will teach you from mistakes and help you get through different trials. They can often strengthen and encourage you to keep fighting.

Now we get to the good part; the friends that are for a LIFETIME. Those are the friends who will never leave you and be with you through thick and thin. *When you run into lifetime friends you will know it.* It isn't necessary to go out looking for them; wait for them to come to you and know that once they come they are there to stay.

My first year in college I surrounded myself with any and everyone and this was sometimes beneficial. Notice I said **SOMETIMES**. All of the other times it wasn't good for me; and those relationship did not uphold the honor code that I intended to live by while in school. I learned my lesson and till this day it is something that I have to pay close attention to, because the last thing I need is someone pulling me down or slowing me down from what needs to be done. The following is an account of the crossroads that I came to in my life while I was fellowshipping with dream-blockers.

One night while I was in my room, I began to pray over my future and the direction that I was to go. I was given a vision and it was quite vivid. I was speechless because it was so deep and real. It felt as if I was actually living out that in which I envisioned. The vision went as follows: I began to pray "Lord I will go where you want me to go and I will do that what've you designed for me to do, and most of all I will say just want you want me to say, when you want it said." Following that prayer came this illustration: A school bus pulled up to my front door step and the bus doors opened wide, and I walked on the bus not knowing what was inside or what was going to come next. The bus pulled off and went to a bus stop and picked up different friends that I had allowed to enter into my life. As the bus continued, I kept seeing different friends, ones I had hung out with and friends I partied with. I even saw some of my prayer buddies! The bus then stopped and some people got off the bus and while others stayed. The bus stopped at red lights, stop signs and yield turns as well. The Lord was saying to me at this point, "Dustin there are things in your life that I have for you to accomplish, but there will be times when everything around you comes to a stop." I continued to get revelation that there were also going to be times when I might feel my dream coming to yield at an intersection. At this point, I proceeded to cry out, "God what is it that you are trying to get across to me?" The response given went something along these lines, "Dustin there are going to come points in your life where you have the choice to bring friends into your life, such as at the bus stop when certain ones came in. What will hinder you will be those who stay in your life or on the bus longer than there ride intended for them to stay."

I want you the reader to think about that just for a second, who have you allowed on your bus and better yet who have you allowed to stay longer than the ride intended. Am I saying that you are supposed to go through friends like underwear? Of course I'm not. I am saying is that you must be careful as to who you allow into your life and the time you allow certain ones in. And when you think about it, it's not always that the person might hurt or harm you, it could be the timing in which it occurs. *Timing can make or break your situation; it can take you over the top or pull you to the bottom.* If you are weak in a certain area in your life, it is good to have friends who might be strong in that area. That way you can balance each other out. I have heard it said, "You can't be around friends who live where you once fell." In other words, if you were once an alcoholic and your best friend is an alcoholic it is going to be hard to overcome that addiction when you are always surrounding yourself with it. When certain ones come in your life in the wrong timing or for the wrong reason they can have a negative effect. They can take you over or pull you all the down. Some might have the ability to make or break you and your dreams. You can become **sidetracked** from your dream and before you know it your dream is gone. I strongly encourage you to check your surroundings and your friends. Most of all be very careful who you tell everything. It's always good to surround yourself with people with such like faith, dreams and goals. The better the people you are surrounded with equals more uplifting and encouragement.

Joseph experienced this with his own family. Because Joseph was the youngest sibling in the family he was looked down upon. It wasn't in Joseph's best interest to share with his brothers the dream God had given him.

> *And he said unto them, Hear, I pray you, this dream which I have dreamed: For, behold, we were binding sheaves in the field, and, lo, my sheaf arose, and also stood upright; and, behold, your sheaves stood round about, and made obeisance to my sheaf. And his brethren said to him, Shalt thou indeed reign over us? Or shalt thou indeed have dominion over us? And they hated him yet the more for his dreams .(Genesis 37:6-8)*

Joseph's own flesh and blood hated his God given dream. They didn't believe in him and were upset that He wanted them to come and help him fulfill his dream. The second point that I want to explore is that you can't expect everyone to help you fulfill your dream. Joseph was positive his brothers would help and support him rather than hinder, hurt and discourage that which he had envisioned because they were his family. He was sure that his own blood would want to help see his dreams come true. But on the contrary, as the story goes on nothing works out for Joseph and in fact things worsen for him. Yet he dreamed another dream and told his brothers

"I have dreamed a dream once more; and behold, the sun and the moon and the eleven stars made obeisance to me. And he told it to his father and to his brethren and his father than rebuked him (Gen 37:9-10)." Joseph was filled with so much joy that he just didn't know how to contain it, and he wanted to let all of his closest loves one know, but the more he told them the more his brothers envied him and the further their relationship grew took a turn for the worse. Because of Joseph's passionate dreams, his brothers intended not only to demolish Joseph dreams, but also Joseph himself ...

Once Joseph's brothers had him alone, they took him and threw him into an empty pit, hoping for the worst. Their intentions were that he would die there and they could live happily ever after. However, Joseph didn't allow anything to hold him down or back, he made it out of that ditch, marching one foot right in front of the next. As time grew, Joseph was faced with some many other trails, and downfalls. Eventually he was thrown in prison sad, depressed, hopeless and confused. Joseph had hit rock bottom, as anything that could have went bad for Joseph indeed did. While sitting in jail he ran into someone else who was a dreamer. Joseph began to gain a little hope as he talked to this random person. In the mist of all of the hell Joseph was put through on the earth, he never forgot about the dream God had given him. As time went on, Joseph and this individual became friends. God began to work on Joseph's behalf things changed for the good and Joseph's dream was beginning to come to past. Eventually, all that Joseph had envisioned came to past.

Overtime with faith, dedication and unwillingness to give up, Joseph received all that God had in store for him. If you remember, Joseph didn't begin to tap into everything God had for him until he was in relationship with that one specific person in the jail. He came into contact with someone with a vision; someone who would believe in him and encourage what he was destined to do. Once Joseph and his friend started planning and organizing their thoughts, things began to work out for them. Why is that? This occurred because they were on the same page and had one purpose. How do you think the story would have ended if Joseph would have given up and yielded to his obstacles? I am more than certain he wouldn't have had the same ending. You might be in a ditch, behind bars or maybe even in your darkest hour; but, God is still there. Keep the dream alive; keep going forth in faith. Never give up or give in. Keep pushing and always have the mindset that the best is yet to come.

I heard it once it said that the richest soil on the ground is graveyards, because so many dreams and visions never came to pass. Many people die left and right with dreams, inventions, foundations, organizations, nation-changing ideas, but they have never come to pass. I am here today to encourage you not to let your dreams die; rather, let the dream rise up inside of you. ***Move it from the back of your closet and place it in your heart. Think about the dream, pray about the dream and most of all act on the dream.*** *Light the fire in your heart to dream again and ignite your vision. See the vision being fulfilled. See you living a life with no limitations, see the dream and those visions will come into full fruition.* Don't allow yourself to only be a dreamer, but keep fighting like Joseph and you will become a dream fulfiller.

Chapter Six
Ignite Your Vision

In the book of Proverbs, Solomon declared: "Where there is no vision people have the possibility of perishing (Proverbs 19:18)." It is always good to have a vision. A vision can begin as an idea in your imagination and then transform into a desire to make it real. The idea then turns into intention and then into will to achieve. It is good to have vision that affects not only you, but also those who come into contact with you. When planning and writing down your vision, begin with the end in mind. See yourself as if the vision has already been fulfilled. You might not be knowledgeable as to when or how the vision is going to come to pass but keep striving at it with your imagination. Imagine things changed and rearranged as the way you envisioned them. Albert Einstein said it best, "Imagination is more important than knowledge." Anyone can be full of knowledge but not everyone has the drive to stick with the vision until the end because of rejection, depression, no dedication or whatever the hindrance. Just know that only you have the power to predict what your future is going to be. **The best way to predict your future is to create your future.** Create it with your vision and define your vision clearly. A well-defined vision leads to satisfaction and a sense of meaning and purpose in life. Daily look over it; work at achieving it and taking the proper steps that are necessary to see it come to pass. Speak over your vision, declare that it shall come into existence, pray about it and most of all stand on it. And once you have done all of that successfully, keep standing.

Ephesians 6:13 (Bible in Basic English)-Take up all the arms of God, so that you may be able to be strong in the evil day, and, having done all STAND and keep your place. I like to add to that: By Faith believe that it will come to pass.

Growing up, the importance of writing down a vision, making it clear and standing on it was stressed greatly. Every time I would have a dream or a vision I was encouraged to write it down. I can't count how many times someone would tell me, "Dustin write it down." I would then break it up into two different segments: I would write down my short-term visions; those things that I can work on today and in the near future to bring my vision to pass. Then I would write down my long-term visions; those are the things that might take a while to complete and require special faith to complete. It is such a relief and comfort to have my goals written out before me. All I had to do was complete each task and then use my faith to see it come to pass. I would often go back to the place in which my goals were written and think to myself, "What can I do this week to ensure myself that I am working towards my God-given dream?" Week after week I would do that and if I didn't see any progress I would work towards it.

Habakkuk 2:2-3 (KJV) says, "...Write the vision, and make it plan upon the tables, that he may run that readeth it. For the Vision is yet for an appointed time, but at the end it shall speak and not lie: though it tarry wait for it because it will surely come." That scripture is telling us the power of writing down the vision and how to be patient and wait for the vision to come. It doesn't mean sit and wait for it to fall out the sky while watching the Simpsons, eating pizza. No, write it down, wait on it, stand on it, do all you can in the natural to bring it pass and with the help of God, the supernatural will begin to occur. There is something that happens when the vision is written down. It gives you better understanding and more focus on what you actually are working toward. When it isn't written down in front of us and we aren't always reminding our self of that which we have set out to complete, we can easily get distracted or side-tracked or even place our vision on the back-burner. Work on keeping the vision on the front burner, with the fire on high. Before you know it, the aroma of achievement will begin to float into the atmosphere. Now, let's create a practical example of writing down the vision:

Let's say that you are a college student who wants to become a medical doctor. What would be a few good short-term goals? First off, if you aren't enrolled, get enrolled in college and take the necessary course load needed for graduation. A long-term vision would be to envision yourself as a student in a medical school. This system shows no favorites and can be utilized by anyone in any situation. The concept of the matter is simply taking one step at time and doing what needs to be done. The more positive steps you take towards your vision the closer you will become to it. Small steps will eventually turn into big steps. 2 Corinthians 9:6 says you "Reap what you sow." If you keep working toward success, and stay dedicated then you will gain success. If you are being lazy about your vision, moving slow, not ever keeping the vision in front of you, then the vision will be following you instead of you following after it. You should get to the point to where the vision is in front of you and you are constantly chasing it—so much so that it becomes apart of you. Get to the place to where you can't stop thinking about it. Let it become an addiction to you.

What happens when someone become addicted to something? They can't sit still or concentrate until they have another dose of what they are addicted to. A person addicted to chocolate isn't going to be completely satisfied until they have had their portion of chocolate for the day. If they don't have it then they are grumpy, upset and begin demanding of some type of chocolate. No matter how hard they try to fight the addiction it is hard to settle without it. The longer the addiction sits the harder it is to break or go without. Well, how much could we accomplish if we allowed our visions to become our addiction? Once we get addicted to our vision, whatever it may be, then nothing can break, hurt, hinder or take us off track of the vision. The longer you stay close to the vision, the harder it will become for the addiction to be broken. Get so close to the vision that it becomes unbreakable, unmovable, unchangeable and eventually fulfilled. Just like the chocolate lover has to have their piece of chocolate in order to feel at peace or rest. Think of different ways and things you can do to feed your addiction in a productive way. My suggestion would be to put action behind the things that you want to see completed.

A vision without action is a daydream. Action without vision is a nightmare, but if you keep your action and vision on the same accord then it can bring to pass your hearts desires. Always know that there is power when you envision things. **The power of having a vision can be described as the ability to seeing beyond our present reality, to create, to invent what does not yet exist, to become what we not yet are.** It gives us the capacity to live out of our imagination instead of our memory. Live, walk, speak, act in the power of the vision that you have. Whatever you put into it you will get out of it. Put your all in to dreaming so one day you can receive it all back.

How a vision does began

"How does a vision begin?" one might ask. I believe that God imparts to you a revelation of His plan for your life. The desires of your heart can also be your vision. The Bible says that God will grant us the desires of our heart if we remain faithful. Some times when things aren't going as we planned or wanted, and when it seems as if the visions or dreams are not working out as we intended, the best thing to do is to speak to it. I don't mean in a low whisper either. We need to get bold and stern saying , "Vision, I command you to line up with the word of God. I send out ministering Angels to go out on my behalf." Romans 4:17 says, "to call those things that are not as though they were." If you want to become a doctor start confessing it right now. That person who is looking to sit in the House of Representatives one day, you can do it. I see that teacher sitting out there. YOU CAN DO IT! No matter what your dream or vision is, start speaking to it today. Don't only speak to it, but every time you speak or confess it, release your faith right then and there. According to James 2:17, "Faith without works is dead."

Beginning a vision is easier than finishing the vision that you have started. Anyone can start, but not everyone that starts actually finishes. One vital key to finishing is persistence. Persistency might be one the most important things you need to complete anything. Think about it, what happens when you lose persistence concerning something? If you are anything like me, you may lose the fire and creative thinking might go away on a particular idea. Before you know it, you have forgotten about it and it becomes like an old piece of fruit that sits on the counter until someone comes and throws it away. Stay persistent and keep the determination. No matter how it looks it shall come to pass. Darwin Hobbs sings a song that says something along these lines ,"God is able to do just what He said He would do, He is going to fulfill every promise in you don't give up on God because He won't give up on you." We can't always do it in our might but once we fully believe in the vision and we have prayed about it than it shall come to pass.

One day as I was studying and reading a book from an amazing motivation speaker today known as Bishop T.D. Jakes, he mentioned something that was so profound— "Vision does not only give meaning and understanding of one's purpose in life, it also gives you wisdom about how to bring those things to pass." After reading that, it opened my eyes to a clearer understand of exactly what it means to have a vision and to pursue that vision in which we have. The vision is what you are expecting to come to past, but as we read from T.D jakes, your vision also gives you wisdom on how to bring it pass. I personally believe that he was saying we need to gain and use wisdom when we are going after our vision. *Wisdom is such a powerful tool we can use to befit us in multiple areas of our lives.*

A great way to gain wisdom is by speaking to those who have walked in the shoes you are trying to wear. Ask questions, find out what was successful and what wasn't successful. Whenever I am given different opportunities to sit and talk with different successful individuals one of my first questions I ask is, "If given the chance to start over what would you do different and why?" I ask a number of little questions that turn into big questions. Before you realize it you will be gaining knowledge and knowledge is power. As you gain this new knowledge you will also be gaining wisdom. There are many ways to get to the top in each and every field; everyone doesn't take the same road. Everyone shouldn't have to fall or bump their head on the same thing time after time again. So if you can gain information on certain things, why not?

For as long as I can remember whenever my mom was having a problem with something or needed advice she would often called my grandmother, known to me as Granny Granny. My mom knew that Granny Granny's opinion was the best. Often I would wonder why that was so. As the years continued to go and time went on Granny Granny and I would have our sit down conversations and she would pour so much into my life. The best part was it always came straight from the heart. Eventually it finally clicked to me why my mom would always called granny when she needed something.

Granny had so much wisdom inside of her that she couldn't help but pour it out to those who came and asked for it. All of her choices good, bad or indifferent were apart of her wisdom. She could tell you so much about how things took place back in the cotton picking days and the different things she had to go through which allowed her to become a stronger woman today. If you were having a bad day I could almost guarantee you that she could have brightened it. She would always say, "Dustin whatever you become, make sure you become the best at it, don't settle until you have become the best, the very best." She would encourage me to stay in school and always make my Heavenly Father smile.

Another one of Granny Granny's well known quotes was: "Remember to keep God first and he shall direct your path, don't take your eyes off of him because he will never take his off you." She would remind me that tests and heartaches would come but if I just keep my eyes stayed on him I will be victorious every time. What was granny doing? She was investing her wisdom inside of me. It was that special wisdom that gave a lot of the family hope, comfort and the reassurance that everything was going to be alright. Granny is now in Heaven smiling down at the family as we walk in the wisdom that we have gained from her life and example. Till this day the words that she has spoken through and over me ring in my ear weekly as I live this life and go out and follow my God given vision.

Today is the day that you can put wisdom, vision, pen and paper together and write down where you expect to see yourself. Hang it on the fridge, in the bathroom mirrors, on the back of your bedroom door. Put it in a place that you visit often and every time you see it read the vision aloud, speak over the vision and act as if the vision you are envisioning has come to pass. See your vision as if your vision is already fulfilled. In the mist of it all, always vision yourself reaching for the sky and if you fall just know that you will land on the stars. With that in mind know that nothing can possibly go wrong and all things will work out for the good of those who trust the lord and act according his word.

Chapter Seven

Your Future Looks Better Than Your Past

"The Past" is something that many of us may be guilty of trying to live in; and often we live there because we are afraid of moving forward. Often, our eyes have not adjusted yet to see the light at the end of the tunnel because the incident still stings of hurt and disappointment. Getting stuck in our past is easier than the forward motion to our future. Therefore, we choose to cling to what we know (the past) and cheat ourselves out of the potential of growth and success in Christ.

It is not healthy to live in a place where you once fell, or where you were hurt. If you don't let it go, it will be the anchor that sabotages your present by either keeping you in the same position causing you to become stagnant or even drag you down to the bottom where the end result can only be depression. Imagine the damage that could be done to your future if your present situation painted a picture of what was to come. *It is hard to paint a colorful picture of a field of flowers using only the color black and when we use our past to dictate our future and present we limit the painting of our life.* The only effective way of dealing with the past is to learn from it and put it behind you and allow it remain there.

Difficult to see your future, when u r staring at your past.

When looking in a rear view mirror what happens? You keep your eyes fixed in to the things that are behind you, when doing this your attention isn't focused to things that are in front of you. The longer you are focused on the things behind you, the more you will become unaware of where you are going, and what is coming your way. I believe sometimes this is the way we are towards our situations in life. We are too focused on what has happened in the past, which is why we aren't noticing the good things God has placed in front of us for our future. Let the past be the past and get ready to walk into your future, free from hurt, harm, danger, and pain. Walk into a new light and let all the darkness remain behind you.

Growing up I loved to run track, and it was required that each runner line up behind the line; if anyone was found in front of the line they were either disqualified or asked to move back. When standing on the line waiting for the gun to go off everything gets quiet to the runners; they forget about all they have been through, they don't think about anything but the race and they listen for the prompt to take off. Once the gun fires, they begin to run their race. Whether they win or lose, they stayed lined up and did what was necessary to start the race, but finishing the race was up to the individual runner. It sometimes gets hard running against the wind, and it may feel like hitting a brick wall if it's a longer race. The main part is that everyone can start with the right qualifications but as the wind is blowing in their faces, discouragement can set in and each runner must decide to keep pushing, fighting and never give up until they have run through to the finish line.

Just imagine putting yourself on that startup line, and forgetting about everything that happened yesterday, last week, a year ago or whatever it is that might be a distraction to you and your destiny. Forget about any hurt, harm, harsh words, actions and friends. *Just think about where you want to go in life.* Have you forgotten about it all yet? If not, take a few more moments and get your mind clear. BANG, the gun just went off, now see yourself running and living the life that God has in store for you to live, keep running, keep running, keep running. Don't stop, you are getting closer to the finish line. Keep running, pace your breathing — your lungs may be burning but you're getting closer and closer. Here you go, the wind is now on your face and as you breeze towards the goal line the wind pushes you backwards as you push forward. You're inching closer... what do you know? You just finished the race!

That was a practice test, now it is up to you to go and complete the real test. I know some things will be harder to forget about than others, but it is all about the first step. As you make that first step to close the door behind you, every other step will be easier. The more you keep stepping into the future the better and brighter it will look. Remember when one door closes, another door opens. *We often look so regretfully at the closed door that we don't see the one that has opened for us. Learn how to let the closed doors stay closed and walk into the new opened door.* There you find success, happiness, peace, joy, love and abundance.

One of the things that I enjoy more than anything is sitting down with my classmates, friends and peers and getting to know who they really are. I take pleasure in gaining understanding of who they truly are by learning their childhood stages and so many other things they are willing to share. One thing I have gained knowledge of is that **everyone has a story**. Some personal stories may be good, bad, ugly, happy or sad. At the end of the day they all have overcome something or could even be in the current process of learning how to overcome. What I am trying to say is everyone had a yesterday, and of course a today. *But don't focus on what happened yesterday when* *there is a tomorrow. Your tomorrow is better than your yesterday. Your latter days are greater than the former days. God's best and blessed days are in front of you and they start with today!* The most amazing part about it all is, all you have to do is go ahead and walk in it. One beneficial thing about a past is you can use it to your advantage by making it the opposition to every disadvantage you faced before — you **learn from it and choose not to revisit it**. You can take all of the anger, frustration and any other negative emotions and turn them into positive actions by doing something creative to help yourself and those around you. The past does not have the power to dictate your future. Learn from it today and it will be a part of your growth for your future.

> **Brethren I count not myself to have apprehended: but this one thing, I do forgetting those things which are behind, and reaching forth unto those things which are before.**
>
> **-Philippians 3:13**

Paul, the writer of the book of the Philippians, explained that it was mandatory for him to forget the things that are behind him in order to reach out after the things that are in front of him. *See, in order to get to what God has in store for us, it is important to reach after it. It isn't going to come to us if we are standing in the hurt, or sitting in the past.* But once we reach out towards our tomorrow and forget about our yesterday, then and only then will you understand and experience just what Paul was saying.

Proverbs 4:18 says, "The path of the righteous is like the first gleam of dawn, shining ever brighter till the full light of day." We may be facing difficulty, but there are brighter days ahead. Personally, I choose to focus on where I am going. That gives me hope and encouragement because, I know that the tough times won't last long. I remember my mother saying this to me, "...there are storms that we all encounter every now and again but the good thing about the storm is that it too shall pass." When a storm comes it doesn't come to stay; the same way it came is the same way it must go. In the midst of the storm simply stand and know that God *is* God.

In Ephesians chapter 6 speaks about the Armor of God, and how we are to dress ourselves for the days ahead. The amour of God is to protect us; it gives us all the tools that will be needed to fight our battles. After it discusses the armor, it goes on to say that after all is done we are to *stand* therefore. When we are going through our storm just know that God has already given us everything we need to win, all we need to do is stand still and know that God is God and always be God. Many people think that since they must stand still, that they don't have to exercise their faith, read the Word, trust or believe. But this is how we show that we are truly fighting the good fight, the fight of faith. This proves that we are digging in, fighting — this is our stand, this is the complete opposite of sitting down spiritually. When we stand still, we are focusing in on the promises of God and choosing to believe what God has forth for us in His Word. It also means that we are not allowing ourselves to become restless, but restfully standing still in and on the word of God. This is how we gain joy and peace in the storm; and by this we ensure that we don't lose our hope or our vision and purpose.

The storm might be raining cats and dogs, but the good thing about almost all storms is that there is an end to them; and at that end, there is always a rainbow. The rainbow is a sign saying the storm is over; it is always a good thing when a rainbow appears. Growing up I always thought that there was gold at the end of the rainbow. To this day I have never had the chance to really find out what is at the end of the rainbow. But one thing I do know: When personal storms try and attack me spiritually, mentally, physically, financially or any other way, I know what to expect that at the end of the rainbow. I am going to look for my pot of gold, and rest knowing that the season has come to an end. I will then enjoy the sun, knowing that the season of rain has left me and I have fully understood what to do and how to stand in the next season.

There is a season to everything we do and have; but some of us stay in a season too long. We get so comfortable in a particular state that we become afraid to experience change. **Well I am here to let you know that change is not bad if you are changing for the right reason.** We should never settle for less than what we are capable of doing or becoming. Fear should never hold us back from a changing season either. Psalm 23:4 says "...Even though we walk through the valley of the shadow of death, the Lord is with us." Notice that it says "walk through." *It doesn't say we are going to pitch a tent and hang out in those hard, dark places.* No, it says we are going through; we're moving forward. What I love the most about that is, even in our darkest hour, in the most rainiest of seasons, when we are fighting the hardest battle and it seems as if there is no one who understands — I've got a secret for you JESUS sees every step, every tear, even during frustration He is right there. When you don't know what to do He is still right there.

Marvin Sapp's wrote a song entitled "Never Would Have Made It." He wouldn't have made it without the hand of the Lord pulling him up every time that he felt low. Some of us can attest to that same thing never would have made it. Just think for a second think about where God has brought you from to where you are now. I don't know about you, but as for me I can't help but shout, jump, run and give Him all the praises that He alone is due. *If it was done once than it will be done again and again and again.*

You Have Everything You Need

Before you were born, God, the great architect of the universe, laid out a plan for your life. He knew what you would need in order to accomplish that plan. He didn't just randomly put something in you. He put in you exactly what you need in order to live a victorious life. Don't ever allow anyone to convince you that you don't have what it takes—that you're not tall enough, you're not talented enough, you don't have the right personality or that you are not smart enough. No, that is an insult to our God. **He has equipped you to fulfill the dreams in your heart.** I personally believe everyone has a dream that they would like to see come to pass. Often times we allow what we hear to affect our dream or better yet, we allow the opposition we're faced with to determine where and what we should be. Philippians 4:13 clearly says, "I **(Dustin Wise)** can do all things through Christ who strengthens me." When I see the letter "I", I make it personal. What people don't seem to understand about the scripture are the words, through Christ. We have a tendency to look at other people's belief or personal stories when we are facing a hard time. He didn't say you could do all things through your mama, your daddy, your boss, your best friend, your sister or your pastor but He said through Christ. Once you start to believe the Word, then rest assure that all things will become possible for you.

Take a stand and declare to yourself that the past is over and all things are made new. We serve the God who makes all things new; all we need to do is follow him forward. All of your hurts, pains, or ungodly decisions can be erased today. It doesn't matter how big or small, important or unimportant, you can't have a better tomorrow if you are always thinking about your today. Always remember no matter what things look like, no matter what other people say, God has equipped you with everything you need to accomplish your dreams. I've heard it said, "Faith begins with stuffing your ears full of cotton." In other words, you can't listen to negative comments because they only drag you down and hold you back. When those negative voices come to you saying, "You're not going to accomplish your dreams. You're not going to be successful." Choose to tune those voices out. Remember, God Almighty—the Alpha and Omega, the Beginning and End—He created you; He equipped you; He called you and He chose you. You are more than enough, and you have everything you need to fulfill the dreams and desires He's placed in you! *I dare you this day to boldly take a stand and march right into your God given dream.* Don't wait until tomorrow, when you can start right now. . Start today, this very hour, this very minute. **Start, start, start, start, start**.........

About The Author

Dustin Wise was born in 1989 in Palmdale, California and at the age of six accepted Jesus Christ as his Savior. Inspired by his mother Mary Wise, Dustin began a life of serving and has been active in the ministry, studying , reading, and growing in the word of God ever since. Dustin is on a mission to inspire and motivate individuals to reach their highest potential in life, living in full purpose, and discovering there God given destiny.

Dustin has been and currently involved in numerous activities such as reaching out to the community, volunteering, holding different workshops as well as speaking the message of hope to his generation. Dustin has spent countless amount of hours working with different burn foundations, burn camps, support groups and outreach programs.

Through his dynamic and informative teaching, Dustin combines biblical principles with practical experiences to motivate the lost, hurt and all others that have let their past control their present. There he inspires, redirects, motivates, strengthens and encourages them to live the life God has intended for them live. This is a victorious life, forgetting the past and moving on into bigger and better blessings.

Dustin answered the call to ministry. He enrolled at Rhema Bible Training Center in Broken Arrow, Oklahoma. There he graduated with an emphasis in pastoral ministry. Dustin is currently a student at Oral Roberts University, where he is studying Interpersonal Organization Communication with a minor in Non-Profit Business.